T0366124

SO FAR FROM HOME

Krystyna Stachowicz Slowikowska Zukian Farley
A Memoir

by Krystyna Slowikowska Farley and Ann Knope

iUniverse LLC
Bloomington

So Far from Home
Krystyna Stachowicz Slowikowska Zukian Farley - A Memoir

iUniverse books may be ordered through booksellers or by contacting:

iUniverse LLC
1663 Liberty Drive
Bloomington, IN 47403
www.iuniverse.com
1-800-Authors (1-800-288-4677)

Because of the dynamic nature of the Internet, any web addresses or links contained in this book may have changed since publication and may no longer be valid. The views expressed in this work are solely those of the author and do not necessarily reflect the views of the publisher, and the publisher hereby disclaims any responsibility for them.

Any people depicted in stock imagery provided by Thinkstock are models, and such images are being used for illustrative purposes only.
Certain stock imagery © Thinkstock.

ISBN: 978-1-4917-0880-4 (sc)
ISBN: 978-1-4917-0881-1 (e)

Library of Congress Control Number: 2013917357

Printed in the United States of America

iUniverse rev. date: 09/27/2013

TABLE OF CONTENTS

Dedicated to all the pilgrims upon this earth who keep the faith having not yet received the promise.

Orlopol

Military Veteran's Settlement of Orlopol in Wolyn
Located two miles southwest of Wisniowiec

5

Krystyna Stachowicz Slowikowska Zukian Farley
New Britain, CT
2011

Preface - By Krystyna Stachowicz Slowikowska Zukian Farley

My Name is Krystyna Stachowicz Slowikowska Zukian Farley. Let me tell you something. That which does not kill you really does make you stronger. Wise words spoken by Elie Wiesel as a result of his experiences during the Holocaust. So many Americans don't know what it means to live anymore. We think we have it so good, that we are free... but we are not free. Everyone here is in such a hurry. No time for God, for country, for family life, no time for friendship, for neighbors and community, no time to vote...only video games, internet, and pilgrimages to Disneyland. If I don't tell my dear husband, Ed, to call his brother, he won't remember to pick up the phone.

I met Ann when we worked together as election officials in New Britain, CT. She turned to me for a conversation when she heard me muttering about how hardly anyone in America votes any more. We became friends and I told her a little of my story. Ann asked me if I had ever written my story. Though I speak many languages pretty well, I find writing in English difficult. Ann volunteered to help me write my story in English so it will not be lost and forgotten by my grandchildren.

How could you really know what happened to the Poles? No one has told you. Let me tell you. The Holocaust effected many people. Elie Wiesel has kept the memory of the Jewish Holocaust alive so that we never forget what happen to the Jews. Let me tell you about the Polish Holocaust. Six million Poles died along side six million Jews, with many people of many cultures, resisting two extremes of the political spectrum, fascism and communism. Neither system works very well.

Nobody knows what really happened because they lied to us, and they buried the truth along with the dead. Who lied to us?

Chamberlain, Churchill, Stalin, Roosevelt, Hitler, and the rest of the European elite, and they lied to themselves. We tend to lose sight of the truth when the truth is too painful. We lose sight of the real objective for life and tend to focus on self-preservation, too afraid to let go of the status quo when the status quo is already kaput.

Oh, I know, they had to do what they had to do, to try and prevent another war, but the war was already on and they refused to acknowledge it. If only we had more courage to stand up to the thugs sooner. If only we all had the courage to take a stand against evil before it backs us into a corner. Poland did not have a choice. With Nazi's to the west, Communists to the east, and betrayers from every background in our midst, good people from every background were threshed and crushed in the middle, while the rest of the world held their breath, hoping the threat would go away. Poland and many good people of Poland, from many cultural backgrounds were brutalized, but not defeated. As our blood and tears poured forth something powerful was brought to birth, the Polish Army in Exile, lead by General Anders in cooperation with England and General MacArthur. In this army, an army without a place to call home, we Poles in Exile helped the Allies begin to push back the Nazi's in Europe at the Battle of Monte Casino. And that was before D-Day.

"Why did you not help the Jews?", the world asks us. "Why did you look the other way?"

Well, six million Poles died trying to take a stand against the Nazi's and the Communists. And many more are still suffering from the struggle. Many, many Poles are still living in exile today, unable to return to their beloved homeland, still searching for missing loved ones, and a place they can truly call home. We tried to stop the aggressors, and help those who resisted, whether Jew, Pole, Russian, German, or Ukraine, but the rest of the world was not ready yet to help us. It was not until our beautiful, fledgling, free nation was completely overrun and plundered that Europe and the West, and, finally, Russia woke up and realized that they were the ones looking the other way.

My family tried to live in peace with those around us in the Kresy - Poles, Russians, Jews, Gypsies, Ukrainians, Catholics, Protestants, and Communists. We tried to resist the gathering storm and sudden eruption of resentment and cruelty. But in the end, because we could not accept the party line and the Nazi's and Communists knew that most Poles would never accept the party line, my family was deported to a slave labor camp in the north of Russia, deep in the vast frozen forests of the Ural Mountains, as were hundreds of thousands of others. As many as 1.5 million Poles were ripped from their homes and sent to slave labor camps and gulags in Russia and Siberia because they could not comprehend the party line let alone cooperate with it. Two thirds of those deported and imprisoned died from the harsh conditions, and hundreds of thousands, like my family, have never been able to return to our homeland. Papa, myself, Chester, Teddy, and Natalie survived and were reunited for a while in England. We lost our beautiful mother, Walentyna, in Uzbekistan to malaria, and my dear elder sister Alice is still missing. We wonder every day if she is still alive, if we will ever find her. We have heard rumors, but to this day, we have not been able to locate her.

And now I live in America, Land of the Free, and Home of the Brave. But we have forgotten our roots, America. We have fallen asleep and do not remember how vigilant we must be to preserve our freedom.

My time on earth will end soon enough. But before I go, bear with me a little while. Let me tell you my family's story. I pray you will listen and wake up; that you will truly appreciate and participate in life, and not settle for just a virtual universe. Even when our life has been scattered to the wind our souls can survive and thrive with passion and love for all that is good in this life. There is so much good in this life. This is the story of a family and how it survived. It could be the story of any family, anywhere; it is the story of your family, too. It is the story of a country, and the heart of a people that survived through the onslaught of those who hoped to crush them, but could not.

Poland and America have a special bond in our love for freedom, personal responsibility, enterprise, and justice. Opposing forces will always try and sacrifice these principles for the sake of power and control, or the status quo. But the light of freedom, creativity, responsibility, and enterprise cannot be completely extinguished. That light will always rise from the ashes like an eagle in the human heart and live on if we nurture it and protect it. It is a precious gift from our Creator.

Come join me in this adventure. Turn the page and experience the courage and spirit of a family and a people who stood in the gap and helped freedom to prevail.

Thank you, Anna, for helping me to write my story.

Cover photograph: Krystyna Stachowicz in 1938 with her cousin Zbigniew Poznachowski, the final happy summer before the invasion of Poland by Hitler and Stalin

CHAPTER 1 - Something Bad Is Going to Happen

The animals knew before the people of the settlements of Wolyn in the Kresy did. Something terrible was coming. The gathering political and economic storm was bringing the peaceful life in the Kresy to a horrible end. Since the end of WWI the Stachowicz family lived in Orlopol, Poland. Andrzej Stachowicz served Austria and Poland well during the first Great War. In 1920 he and many of his comrades were each given two horses and some land in what was at that time Poland's southeastern province, known as the Kresy. Andrzej Stachowicz married Walentyna Poznachowska, an accomplished musician, seamstress, and teacher, the love of his life; and together over the next eighteen years, they built a beautiful life together raising a family of five strong, healthy children on thirty-three acres of land he received for his military service.

In 1939, unbeknownst to the Stachowicz family, the Allies sat by and allowed Hitler and Stalin to divide Poland in two. The Molotov-Ribbentrop Pact gave western Poland to Germany and eastern Poland to Russia. Imagine, with the stroke of a pen on that fateful August day the freedom loving people of Poland were placed on the altar of the status quo to try and prevent another World War, a war that could not be avoided if freedom was to be preserved. The young Polish Constitution that was re-established after World War I, and so similar to the American Constitution, was cherished by most everyone in the Kresy, helping many different cultures to live in peace. Many of Poland's leaders and intellectuals made great effort to welcome all and protect the individual rights of everyone. Now the fledgling hope of the Polish people was about to be tossed aside and trampled underfoot by fascist and communist army boots. The Poles in the eastern provinces had to be most vigilant about protecting their hard won freedoms. The eastern borderlands of Poland were constantly threatened by Bolshevik ambitions, and the

Poles pushed the communists back from their land on more than one occasion between WWI and WWII against tremendous odds. With Hitler on the horizon, Russia partnered with Ukrainian Nationalists that were sympathetic to the communist ideology and who did not want the Poles or the Jews living amongst them. With the Ukraine on board, the Russians made a truce with Hitler. The Stachowicz family, and those around them in the Kresy suffered brutal consequences.

Two weeks before the Russians marched in to take control of the Kresy, the animals in the stable began to behave in strange ways. The chestnut horse kicked her longtime companion, the black and white cow, and tore off the cow's beautiful long horn. The little black dog that always protected the barnyard animals in spite of his mean temperament killed nine of the family geese and piled them up, nice and neat, at the doorstep, one on top of the other. Krystyna heard her mother Walentyna say, "Something bad is going to happen." Her mother was right.

Just a few weeks later many Ukrainian Nationalists, in cooperation with the Russian Communists, turned against the Polish military veterans' settlements in the Kresy, and against the Jews. The Russian tanks rolled into the Kresy in September of 1939; and by February 10th, 1940, the entire Stachowicz family, Andrzej, Walentyna, and their five children, Alice, Krystyna, Teddy, Chester, and Natalie were loaded into cattle cars for a 30 day nightmare journey into the frozen forests of the Ural Mountains in Russia, to perform slave labor for Stalin's ambitions, never to see the Kresy again, where Andrzej and Walentyna worked so hard to create a home and productive farm for their family and community.

Krystyna, who had turned fourteen that summer, knew something was wrong when she overheard her parents whispering, trying to figure out where to hide food and supplies from the Russian soldiers and the Ukrainian police. The joy of summer days spent talking, singing, dancing, playing and laughing with friends and family were replaced with worry and fear as the newly formed Ukrainian police began to make the lives of the Poles and the Jews in the area impossible. The joy began to be replaced with sadness and fear in everyone's faces.

Shortly after Krystyna's fourteenth birthday in August 1939, a Ukrainian man confronted Krystyna as she left a dance festival; he grabbed at her breast. Krystyna was so shocked that she slapped him hard in the face and ran home in tears. Her mother, Walentyna, admonished her for the retaliation, telling her that she needed to be more careful lest the family suffer reprisals. But Krystyna, in defiance of the humiliation, reminded her mother that no one should be allowed to behave the way that man did. It was in total opposition to the Golden Rule and her strict Catholic upbringing. It made no sense to her at all. It was madness.

Flour, cabbage, cheese, and spirituous began to disappear. Horses, and cows were mutilated in the dark of night while out to pasture in the once tranquil meadows; the tails were cut off for sifters during harvest time, but now the tails were hacked off completely and the livestock was left in the fields to bleed to death and die from infection. Jews and Poles were marched off for execution by Russian and Ukrainian firing squads; women were raped, newborns ripped from their mothers' arms, dashed against the walls. "Don't worry, you will have another one." Having just turned fourteen on August 19th of 1939, Krystyna, and her brothers and sisters, aged five to sixteen years old, had no idea what to make of the sudden changes, or why certain Ukrainians came into the settlements all of a sudden with such contempt and harsh treatment.

Father was so good to everybody; it was not their Ukrainian neighbors that they worked with side by side for so many years that harmed them. It was the ones who lived further away, who did not know them, that began to terrorize the people of the settlements of Wolyn nestled between Wisniowiec and Wola Korybutowiecka. The days of lighting the fire on the Sabbath at the home of Krystyna's dearest and best friend Misha, a beautiful Jewish girl, and classmate who lived in Wisniowiec, were over. Krystyna would never see Misha again. Now it was time to figure out how to stay alive in the midst of this sudden manifestation of national and economic struggle, and rising ethnic hatred. The communist regime of Russia was ruthless, as were the Ukrainian Nationalist police.

Mother did what she could to help hide and protect neighbors and friends suddenly targeted for execution, but soon Krystyna's family also became targets when the Russians crossed the border into their beloved Poland that September. With the stroke of a pen wielded by total strangers, Hitler, Stalin, Chamberlain, and Roosevelt all in agreement, their life was no longer their own. The communists moved into the Kresy, forbade the Polish language in the schools, or talk of God and the Catholic Church. Now Russian was the official language, and anyone who believed in God was considered a fool. By February of 1940, less than six months after the Molotov-Ribbentrop Pact was signed, the Stachowicz family found themselves on a transport to a Russian forced labor camp to harvest lumber for the Russian military all because someone, somewhere made a deal. The night before they were forced into exile, they were wondering what to do about the hidden flour that was going bad. Not realizing what was coming, Father decided to go to the nearby Ukrainian village of Kuniniec to make a batch of spirituous so the flour would not go to waste. Krystyna begged him not to go into the village that night, but Father and Mother went, assuring her that her older sister Alice would take care of her and her younger brothers and sister. Andrzej and Walentyna returned just before dawn on the morning of February 10th and placed the big glass gallon jars of alcohol on the kitchen floor. Just as they climbed into bed and were falling asleep, at 6:00 AM, the Russian soldiers with Ukrainian police startled the exhausted family, pounding on the door, and hollering, "Get your stuff! You are going for an interview!"

Father opened the door and men in uniform with guns came into the kitchen.

The soldier glared at Father and pointing to the jars of freshly distilled spirituous on the kitchen floor demanded, "What is that?!"

Krystyna boldly intervened with the first of many lies, saying to the soldier, "That is boiled water."

"Why is the water boiled?" The soldier asked roughly.

"We get water from the well. Mother insists that we boil it."

The soldier greedily eyed Walentyna. She was beautiful. "Who is this?!" he demanded, thinking she was one of Andrzej's daughters.

Andrzej stepped toward the soldier with clenched fists saying, "She is my wife!"

The soldier backed down, spit on the floor and repeated the command to get their stuff. Krystyna wrapped the jars of spirituous in cloth, and ripped the family sewing machine out of its cabinet. She did not know at that moment why she grabbed the alcohol and the sewing machine 'to go for an interview,' but both would come in handy as they began their struggle to survive. Krystyna also grabbed the beautiful ceramic cross from off the sitting room wall and wrapped it carefully in a blanket, praying for courage as they were forced out into the freezing winter dawn. Father and Mother gathered the family and a few meager belongings into the sledge along with Krystyna, the spirituous and the sewing machine. Leaving the animals and their once beautiful life behind they did not realize as they set out on that bitter cold snowy morning that they were headed into the unknowns of exile on a freight train that awaited them in Horynka. Had they known what was coming they would have taken more food and supplies but the soldiers did not give them that opportunity.

They traveled 30 miles to the train station by sledge as more and more sleds joined the caravan guarded by Russian soldiers and Ukrainian police. At least they were all together. Father would know

16

what to do and Krystyna was determined to help any way that she could, even if it meant at times she had to lie to help keep her family alive. She lied to the soldier about the spirituous. Mother hated lying, and never did. Krystyna's lie came in handy when the men on horseback and walking with the caravan found themselves freezing from the cold. Andrzej saw how cold Krystyna was and jumped off his horse and into the sledge to warm her. Krystyna smiled and told her father that she brought the spirituous. Before long the men were lining up behind their sledge for sips of the alcohol to warm their blood in the forty below zero temperatures. It was a particularly harsh winter that year in the Kresy. The snow piled up above the roof tops and covered all but the tops of the trees. Many on this unexpected journey suffered because of it, especially the elderly and the very young. The thirty mile journey by sledge to Horynka took most of the day and was just the beginning. By the time they arrived at the train station in Horynka, the jars of spirituous were empty.

There was no interview in Horynka. As soon as they arrived Krystyna and her family were loaded onto a box car with their few belongings. German planes flew overhead buzzing the migrating convoys as they spied on the Russian troupe movements. Over 250,000 others from all around the Kresy had also been rounded up by the Russian military and Ukrainian police on that bitter cold February night. This was one of many round-ups to come in Poland over the next few terrible years. Sixty people to a boxcar, each car was divided into two compartments. Each compartment held thirty travelers, herded like cattle. Wooden bunks in each half of the box-car, each wooden slab slept 10 people, a wood stove in the center of the car for heating and for cooking what little food was available, and for added humiliation, a hole in the floor was now their toilet.

Within two hours of the Stachowicz family's arrival at Horynka, as the trains jerked forward and began to move, the people held their breath with fear and perplexity, not knowing where they were going, or what was happening to them, or why they were being forced to leave their beds and be moved like cattle into an a cold and bitter unknown.

The Russian and Ukrainian authorities knew where these unsuspecting people were going. They had been planning the deportations for months – even as they were promising the Poles that they would not have to leave their homes. It was very important that the 'relocations' be carried out 'quickly and in an orderly manner'. Under martial law, all weapons were confiscated. Anyone who resisted was subject to arrest and in many cases immediate execution. Russia and Germany divided Poland in two with the reluctant but calculated cooperation of the Allied powers, Churchill, Roosevelt, and Chamberlain. They knew Hitler and Stalin were a serious threat to Europe and hoped that by sacrificing Poland they would prevent a wider war. As events quickly unfolded they soon realized the wider war was upon them and the treaty with Hitler only emboldened the Nazi ambitions.

With no electricity, radio or TV available in the Kresy settlements, the Stachowicz family had no idea what was really happening until it was too late. There were rumors and warnings from Ukrainian neighbors to hide from time to time that autumn, and they would hide supplies, or flee to the potato fields at night to sleep; but there was no reliable information about what was coming, only the lies published in the newspapers or broadcast on radios in the city of Wisniowiec about how Russia was in Poland to help them. As soon as the pact between Hitler and Stalin was signed on August 23rd of 1939, the Germans invaded western Poland. In September Russian soldiers marched into the Kresy from the north and the east. They immediately began to round up the intelligentsia, the Polish military officers, teachers, priests, nuns, university professors, and anyone who did not cooperate. Many of these people, Poles, Jews, and anyone who resisted were executed at prison camps like Katyn in March of 1940, or sent to German concentration camps, or to the gulags in Siberia. The Russians blamed the Nazi's for the slaughter, but the West is finally realizing it was Stalin that decimated the best and brightest of the Polish people from the Kresy.

Krystyna's mother and father continued to work the farm that autumn of 1939, but began hiding supplies as the military and the Ukrainian police started confiscating everything. Father, a member of the Polish Army Reserves from 1923 to 1939, and therefore already on a list of potential 'anti-soviet elements', kept a low profile, trying to help the WWI veteran military families of the settlement of Orlopol and the settlements nearby. Father was at the well in the nearby city of Wisniowiec watering the horses when a young Jewish boy went by skipping and whistling. A Polish officer came out of the tavern all drunk and disheveled, and spied Andrzej at the well with the horses as the young boy took refuge behind Andrzej. The officer, staggering and drunk, approached Andrzej yelling at him and accusing him of whistling, slapping Andrzej hard on the face. Andrzej put down the bucket, grabbed the chain attached to the bucket, and then grabbed the drunk Polish officer by the collar, and 'gave the officer a good whopping.'

The officer fell down to the ground as the people looked on in horror, shouting, "Stachowicz, What are you doing?!!"

Father said, "What?!! This soldier behaves like a pig. He needs to learn some manners."

The Jewish boy was able to run away. Andrzej was taken in for questioning but the police soon let him go because the officer was drunk.

When Germany overran Poland in the west, there was an influx of Jews from Chemielnik. They fled to Wolyn from their village that had been their home for hundreds of years. The Jews arrived in Wolyn hoping that they would find refuge. Soon they realized that they were hated by the Ukrainian Nationalists even more than by the Germans. One day that autumn Mother spied through the window as she was working in the kitchen and saw Russian soldiers and Ukrainian police on the road to Wisniowiec outside their home taking three Jewish men at gunpoint to be executed. She ran out of the house to the road and told the soldiers that these men worked for her in the fields and she needed them for the harvest. Walentyna did not know these Jewish men, but she knew they would be killed if she did not intervene. The soldiers reluctantly released them into Walentyna's custody and she hid them on the farm and fed them for three months until they found another place of refuge.

It was only when the Stachowicz family was loaded on the train that they realized that their life in Orlopol, their beloved home since Andrzej and Walentyna were married, and where Walentyna gave birth to their five children, was over. Would they ever see their home again? Everything was left behind, the settlement, the farm, their warm home carefully covered in straw for the winter, the animals, the seeds drying in the beautiful vases above the woodstove intended for next year's planting. All was a fading memory as the trains began to roll into the deep wilderness of Russia.

Back Cover: Illustration of the Stachowicz home in Orlopol drawn by Krystyna's sister Natalie Rak in 2013. Krystyna remembers it was surrounded by cherry trees. Her brother Chester fell from the tall one in the front yard by the road.

CHAPTER 2 - And So We Sang

The freight car was dark and cold. The only warm place was right next to the stove. The only light came from the embers in the stove and one small window near the top of the box car. Everyone was cold, hungry, afraid and perplexed.

"Father, where are we going?"

"Mother, where are they taking us?"

"Is there anything to eat? I am so hungry. It is so cold."

Krystyna's mother was a musician. She graduated from the Russian college. She could play any instrument and loved to play guitar, piano, accordion and harp. She taught the children to read and write Polish. She even hired a Polish teacher to come to the home to teach in Polish when the Russians banned the Polish language in the schools. Father was adventurous but at the same time pragmatic. Born in Budki, Poland, March 10, 1898, and named Andrzej Stokowicz, he ran away from home at the age of 14, because he had a difficult relationship with his stepfather. He left behind his mother and his sister, renouncing any inheritance, leaving his claims to his sister. He found work in Austria at the home of a wealthy man who took a shine to Andrzej, so much so, that he wanted him to marry his daughter. Well, that did not sit well with Andrzej so he stole away again into the night, and this time, he joined the Polish military. Now sixteen years old, he served an officer in Austria. Andrzej worked with the animals, becoming a skilled equestrian with a special touch when it came to the horses.

When Andrzej joined the Polish Army during WWI his commander changed his name from Andrzej Stokowicz to Andrzej Stachowicz, saying to him, "What kind of name is Stokowicz? From now on you are Stachowicz!"

At the end of WWI Andrzej met Walentyna and they married against Walentyna's parents' wishes. Her parents were wealthy and wanted her to marry someone more worthy of her social standing, but Walentyna fell in love with Andrzej and that was that. She joined Andrzej and built a beautiful life with him for the family in one of many experimental agricultural settlements in eastern Poland. The settlement was called Orlopol; it was in Wolyn, the eastern most province of the Kresy, the tip of Poland's spear against the Bolsheviks in Russia. Poland was deeply involved after World War I in researching and experimenting with ways to improve agriculture and produce more food for the people. At the end of WWI many truly wanted to beat their swords into productive plowshares.

Every night after a hard day's work, Mother would lie down on the bed and each of the children would take turns reading in Polish. She would always correct the children so they would learn to pronounce the words perfectly. Krystyna's sister Natalie, the youngest in the family, even learned by heart the beloved Polish poem titled The Return of the Father (Powrot Taty), by Adam Mickiewicz. She was five years old and could recite it beautifully. Mother was also an accomplished seamstress, and this is how Krystyna learned to sew so well. Krystyna loved to sew and even made a beautiful outfit for her baby sister Natalie. She was mad at her older sister Alice one day so she made it from one of Alice's beautiful black uniforms that Alice wore to school. This got Krystyna into big trouble with Alice and with Mother; but Mother was so proud of how well it came out that she bragged to everyone about the good workmanship that Krystyna did, showing them the perfect collar, and well-crafted sleeves.

There were no instruments on the box car, but that did not discourage Mother. She had always encouraged the family to sing and dance and participate in shows at village and settlement gatherings and at the schools. There were many plays and recitals in the settlement. Mother always helped with rehearsals and costumes. She insisted that the children fully participate in the activities; so now that they were in the boxcar with nothing else to do, Mother insisted that everyone sing. And that is what they did. All the way to Russia

23

they sang as much as they could; church songs, hymns, folk songs; anything to take their minds off the dark unknowns, the cold and the hunger. This irritated the Russian soldiers to no end, but they could not stop the Poles from singing.

Alice, Krystyna, Teddy, Chester, and Natalie were comforted that the family was together. They did their best to keep occupied on the journey but it was difficult. Alice was the eldest and tried to keep an eye on the younger ones. Krystyna was second born and was not as responsible as Alice. Alice and Krystyna were constantly competing with each other for Andrzej and Walentyna's attention, playing tricks on each other and getting into trouble. Krystyna did her best to annoy Alice at every opportunity. Teddy was the middle child and firstborn son. He was well behaved and studied hard. He made every effort to obey his parents and please his mother, Walentyna.

Chester, born two years after Teddy, was adventurous, fearless, and loved his Father. He shadowed Andrzej whenever he could and learned how to handle the horses and livestock though he was still very young, having turned ten in 1939. Only Andrzej and Chester could get near the Chestnut horse. She was a very special horse, and too skittish to trust anyone else. Not even the demons who cut off the tails of the livestock in the night in the fields could get close enough to harm her. She was one of the few horses who kept her tail. The Russian soldiers demanded that the chestnut horse be brought to the village to be harnessed to grind the wheat at the village mill. Father complied and brought the chestnut horse to help with the work. Chester had other plans. The chestnut horse was his and no one was going to confiscate her and take her from him. He went to see the horse at the mill and when no one was looking he placed a burr under her yoke. The chestnut horse went wild with rage, broke the yoke and ran back to the barn in Orlopol. A soldier came to the house later that day to get the horse back. Andrzej offered to help the soldier retrieve the horse from the barn, knowing

24

she would not let the soldier near her. The soldier refused Andrzej's help saying he knew how to handle the horse. After five minutes the soldier still did not come out of the barn. Walentyna said Andrzej better go check on the soldier. When Andrzej got to the stable, the horse was stomping on the soldier, ready to kill him. Andrzej pulled the horse off of the soldier and the soldier left knowing that nobody would be confiscating that horse for their purposes. She trusted no one but Andrzej and Chester. Even Walentyna was unable to ride her. When she tried, the horse became skittish and threw Walentyna to the ground. The horse did not hurt her, but only Andrzej and Chester could handle her.

Natalie, now sitting in the cramped boxcar at the tender age of five, was the youngest and Krystyna always called her 'My Baby.' This journey would be especially hard on Natalie. To this day she does not like to talk about it.

Every night the soldiers would take a head count on the train to be sure no one tried to escape. Chester, unlike level-headed Teddy, was a rascal from the day he was born. Even this journey into the unknown could not change his nature. When the soldiers took the head count, Chester would stand on one side of the divider in the boxcar to be counted and then would sneak to the other side of the divider to be counted again, so the soldier's count was always one too many. Needless to say Chester got into trouble with Walentyna when she found out.

Along the way the trains would stop for water and supplies. The train stations were not like here in America. The Russian train stations were huge, with rows and rows of train tracks as far as the eye can see, sometimes, two to four miles wide. When the trains stopped designated deportees were allowed to go to the churches, now converted to magazines, and filled with blankets and black bread to re-supply the transports. Each cattle car had two buckets for water for drinking and washing for sixty people. They would take the buckets to the pumps to fill them and carry them back to the train. They would have to hurry to get back to the trains before they started rolling again, or risk being left behind in the wilderness; or worse, be executed for 'trying to escape.' At one stop, a sixteen year old girl with beautiful long blond braids crawled under a railroad car in an effort to hurry back to her boxcar. As she crawled under the train, the train started rolling without any warning and her head was cut off. Her head rolled and bounced down the embankment with her long beautiful braids still attached, tumbling like a ball. Nobody stopped. Nobody dared. The soldier just stood there with a gun to prevent anyone from going to her body to bury it. Krystyna still carries that terrible picture in her mind's eye to this day. She will never forget that beautiful girl crushed by the train, her head separated from her body with no mercy, no concern, no burial.

One night when the train stopped for water, the rest of the family was asleep, but Krystyna was wide awake, unable to keep her mind from racing. A soldier told her to grab the water buckets. There were three buckets available, when there should only have been two. Krystyna grabbed all three buckets and followed the soldier to the water pump. The soldier told Krystyna to pump the water and fill the buckets. Krystyna pretended not to know how. The soldier spit on the ground and pumped the water filling the three buckets. He told Krystyna to carry the buckets, but Krystyna pretended they were too heavy. The soldier was angry but carried the three buckets back to the freight car. Krystyna's mother, Walentyna, woke up and was very worried that something bad might have happened to Krystyna. When Krystyna returned to the freight car with the soldier and the three buckets of water, Walentyna decided to cut Krystyna's long dark hair to protect her from unwanted attention and to combat the lice that was beginning to torment everyone.

The trains would lumber along for hours and hours, rocking and clicking with monotonous rhythm, occasionally stopping to drop off cars and pick up others as it steamed its way through the bitter cold landscape. There was no place to go if anyone tried to escape, only miles and miles of vast winter wilderness, snow and dark forests as far as the eye could see. The deportees simply endured the nightmare; they had no other choice.

The bread was black and watery, and was rationed carefully. The authorities that planned and executed the deportations had strict guidelines on how much to give to each deportee. The objective was to feed them as little as possible to keep them weak, and less apt to rebel, without killing them so they would be able to work when they arrived at their destinations. Excerpts from NKVD documents go into great detail regarding policies and procedures for dealing with 'anti-Soviet elements' selected for deportation, and labor camp organization and rules. Basic Order No. 001223, dated October 11, 1939, deals with 'Instructions on Deportations' designated as 'strictly secret' and 'of great political importance.' The many documents related to the deportations were prepared and approved well in advance of the events of 1939 and 1940; even as the communist authorities were promising the Poles in the Kresy that they were safe and would not have to leave their homes. Many died along the way to the labor camps and gulags from the cold, starvation, dysentery, and typhus. Bodies would be stacked near the freight car door and then tossed into the wilderness when the trains stopped for re-supply or re-direction. One little baby in Krystyna's car died just a few days into their journey because her mother had no more milk in her breasts to give to the child.

Families from what was once eastern Poland were transported to hundreds of camps across the Russian wilderness from Uzbekistan to Siberia. Before Stalin was done 1.5 million Poles were 'relocated.' The Stachowicz family's unwanted journey brought them to Molotowskaja Obl. Dobranski Rejon Nikulinski Siel Sowiet, a camp on a tributary to the Wolga River. When the train stopped, they were loaded into sleds for a trek deep into the forest. It was now March 14th, 1940. They had been on the train for over thirty days and thirty nights with no idea where they were being taken.

Thoughts of food filled their imagination, wondering where the next morsel of bread would come from.

As Krystyna relayed this story to me I could only imagine how difficult this sudden turn of events was for her family and for the hundreds of thousands of others uprooted from their homelands. As perverse as the situation was, Krystyna and her family were better off in exile than many of their neighbors who remained behind. Poles still in the Kresy after this first relocation of 250,000 were brutalized, raped, murdered, and sent to executions. The Ukrainian Nationalists wanted no vestige of Polish blood left in what they believed to be their land. Several more deportation round-ups took place in the Kresy between 1940 and 1943. Then came the massacre of the remaining Poles in Wolyn. Well documented, every day more and more records of those terrible events are coming to light as Russia finally admits its culpability in the removal of the Poles from what was once eastern Poland. Wolyn was the eastern most part of The Second Polish Republic after WWI, an area that had gone back and forth between Russia and Poland over many years, heavily disputed and desired because of its fruitful, agricultural heritage and production. From 1943 to 1945 it became a killing ground of ethnic cleansing as the Ukrainian Nationalists attacked the remaining Poles and Jews, mainly by night, killing the inhabitants of the Polish and Jewish villages and settlements right down to the last man, woman and child. Ukrainians married to Poles during that terrible time were ordered to kill their spouses and their children, or also be killed, in the mad attempt to purge the area of any memory of the Poles. To this day, Krystyna cannot return to Orlopol. Orlopol no longer exists. Wolyn is now part of the Ukraine, handed over to the Russians in 1945 at the Yalta Conference. If she were to attempt to return to the area she would be arrested as an 'anti-Soviet.'

Walentyna - Krystyna's only remaining photograph of her mother.

CHAPTER 3 - The Camp

The Stachowicz family was fortunate that Andrzej was allowed to remain with his family. He was not singled out as a criminal and separated from his family like many other fathers who were put on separate trains and sent to Gulags in Siberia, or in some cases sent to be executed. Andrzej was a hard worker. His gift with horses was well known among the villages in the Kresy, and enabled him to meet or exceed his quotas in the labor camp in Russia on a regular basis. This provided additional rations for him and his family. Perhaps this is why over the next two years, in the midst of a strange and harsh existence, Andrzej, Walentyna and all five of their children were able to at least survive. Even with the extra rations it was barely enough to subsist on let alone satisfy. For the next two years, until June of 1942, they would work in the camp, cutting lumber, forced to meet strict quotas or go without food. The winter was cold and harsh but the work had to be done or they would die. Andrzej, Walentyna, sixteen year old Alice, and Krystyna, having turned fourteen back in August, joined the work crews. Children under the age of fourteen were not allowed to work so Teddy aged twelve, Chester aged ten and Natalie, only five years old, attended the orphanage, a school run by their Russian captors, where they were immersed in communist doctrine. Because children did not work their rations were even smaller than the meager rations of those who did, and consisted of 200 grams of bread per day according to NKVD documents.

Krystyna was glad to work for the little bit of extra food, black watery bread, hot tea with hard candy for sweetening, watery soup with potato peels, and an occasional fish head. But always, there was never enough. Every waking moment was filled with thoughts of how to stave off the hunger. Krystyna took every opportunity to steal food when she could. Mother did not approve, but the children were starving.

When they arrived at the camp Krystyna remembers seeing Tatar ladies. The Tatar ladies were kind and helpful. Their people, too, were forced to work in the camps by the Soviets over many years, and they knew how to survive the harsh conditions. The Tatars are a hearty people who have lived in Eastern Europe and in Russia for many generations from the Kresy to Siberia. A small unit of Tatars lived in the Kresy and had helped the Poles beat back the Russians after WWI. In the labor camp, the Tatars showed the Stachowicz family how to face the deadly winters teaching them to make foot coverings called lapcie made of braided bark strips. Leather shoes would not keep their feet warm in this kind of cold, so the workers bundled their feet in cloth and wrapped the braided bark around the cloth. The shoes were like moccasins with long strings of braided bark to hold the cloth in place. They also showed them where potatoes grew along the river banks, and where to gather berries and wild mushrooms during the brief Russian wilderness summers.

Krystyna's job was to help the Tatar ladies carry large boxes filled with wood blocks to the tractors. The tractors were powered by steam produced by burning the wood blocks. It took two people to carry the large boxes filled with wood blocks. Krystyna always carried at the back of the large boxes and the Tatar ladies helped her because it was hard for her. Father harnessed and worked the horses that dragged the logs to the river for transport downstream. When the summer melt came the logs would flow down the river to factories in the South. Mother and Alice helped strip the branches from the tree trunks when they were felled. The branches would be burned and the trunks were dragged to the river. Andrzej was frequently given horses that would lie down and refuse to work as soon as the big leather harness was put on. He was very careful to be sure that no soldiers were around before he gave the horses a good whopping to force them to work. If the soldiers caught him whipping a horse, he would be executed. It was ok to treat people harshly, but not a horse. Andrzej knew if he did not get that horse to work his family's rations would be cut, and they would starve to death. When a horse did not want to work, the horse would simply lie down in the snow, harness and all. The workman would have to remove the big leather harness and then get the horse up, put the harness back on the horse, and hope that the horse would not lie down again. One day when no one was looking Andrzej whipped a horse good and hard with the harness still on it until it got up and pulled the logs. Andrzej regularly met his quota. Because he was good at what he did, Andrzej was able to earn boots called walonki made of camel's hair. A co-worker, a friend of the family, who was deported with them from a settlement near Orlopol, was not so successful. He was caught hitting a horse in an effort to get it to work. But when the soldiers came to arrest the man, he was already dead from starvation.

Krystyna remembers that it was so cold that her eyes would freeze shut if she blinked. She suffered from chicken blindness due to their poor diet and Alice would lead her around the camp by the hand. Once Alice led her in the wrong direction and Krystyna fell in the deep snow and was completely buried. Alice laughed so hard that she got into trouble with Mother. A Russian lady gave Krystyna some liver to put into her soup. She told Krystyna to let the steam go up into her eyes and then eat the liver. Fortunately, Krystyna's eyes got better so she could see. Others were not so fortunate.

In December of 1940, Krystyna found some potato peels and Mother made a soup for their first Christmas Eve in the labor camp. It was not much, but they were thankful to have it. Because the portion of bread given to the children that were too young to work was so meager, Mother and Father always shared what they had with Teddy, Chester and Natalie. That Christmas Eve Krystyna sat quietly and reminisced of Christmases past. It had been a happy time when the family would gather around the table in Orlopol for a lovely meatless feast with Mother's wonderful cooking and candy and sweets. The youngest in the family would go outside and watch for the first star in the night sky and run into the house and announce it so the meal could begin. They would then pass the wafer thin oplatek around the table. Each person would break off a small piece and then pass the wafer to the person next to them. After dinner they would decorate the tree and then walk the two mile path to church to attend midnight mass eager to sit with Grandfather, Walentyna's Papa, and with Walentyna's brother, Uncle Felix. Seeing them on Christmas was always special. In those happy days Grandfather and Uncle Felix lived in the nearby village of Narutowicze in Wolyn. For the Poles, Christmas was not about buying presents; it was about making special decorations as gifts for each other to hang on the tree; and most of all it was about the birth of Jesus. As she was re-membering Krystyna took a piece of birch bark and made a postcard. She wrote a note to her Uncle Felix back in Poland saying that they were 'alright and happy' in their new land. That was all she could write because all mail going in and out of the camp was screened by the Russian military. Her Uncle Felix kept the postcard and showed it to Krystyna many years later when she visited Warsaw just before Western Poland regained some independence with the collapse of the USSR.

    The summers in the Ural were short, and though warmer, summers presented different challenges.   Rats, lice, insects, all added to the discomfort. The rats competed with the deportees for the bread. The workers would have to hang their meager portions of bread from the rafters wrapped in cloth to try and keep the rats from eating it. Andrzej would take the children into the woods to gather mushrooms and berries, but they had to watch out for bears. Krystyna knew of a place by the river where potatoes were planted. She decided to ride a horse to the river and steal some. On the way a bear startled the horse; the horse turned tail and ran. Krystyna had to hold on for dear life all the way back to the camp. One day while gathering berries the family came across a shed in the woods. Inside Andrzej found the skeleton of a man chained to a table; the man probably starved to death in that terrible place many years before. Andrzej sent the children back to their cabin and he buried the man's bones the next day.   Walentyna put the sewing machine that Krystyna brought on their journey to good use. She sewed and repaired clothing for the German prisoners that were kept by the Russians in a nearby Gulag. Walentyna also told fortunes using playing cards. She told the Commandant that he would soon be a single man. Everyone knew he and his wife were not happy. Sure enough, the Commandant's wife left him for someone else. He just laughed it off. He knew what was coming.

Life in the camp was difficult. With the logging going on, there was plenty of wood to burn, and water to drink, but never enough food to eat, or clothes to wear, and keeping warm, clean and free of rats and lice in the drafty crowded barracks made life particularly unpleasant. Everyone kept their head down and worked for fear of starvation or, even worse, reprisals. This was hard for Krystyna and her brothers and sisters to understand having lived such a happy life in Orlopol. The first winter in the camp took its toll on many of their neighbors from the Kresy; many of them died from the terrible conditions, or were executed for breaking rules or angering the guards. The brief summer was coming to an end quickly with another ten months of bitter cold at the door.

CHAPTER 4 - God Does Not Want to Stay Here Anymore

In March of 1942, after two years of harsh conditions in the camp, Krystyna became very ill and could not work. The cabins were constructed from logs and were elevated above the snow on stilts so the wind blew through the floor boards which made sleeping on the floor cold and uncomfortable. Sleeping on the cold floor took a toll on Krystyna. She could not move or walk because the pain in her back and legs was so bad. The rest of the family went to work and to school and Krystyna stayed behind in the cabin to sleep. A soldier pounded on the door and entered the cabin. He asked Krystyna why she was not at work. She told him she was sick.

The soldier spit on the floor, and pointed to the ceramic crucifix on the wall saying, "What is that?! Is He going to feed you?"

Krystyna responded, "He must feed me; you certainly don't."

The soldier told her to take the crucifix off the wall.

Krystyna, too sick to move, said, "If you want the crucifix off the wall, you take it down."

The soldier spit on the floor and walked out, slamming the door behind him. About half an hour after the soldier left, the beautiful black ceramic crucifix with the pink Jesus slid down the wall and shattered on the floor. Only the loop and the nail remained on the wall. Krystyna's mother came back from work and saw the broken crucifix on the floor. She was upset and asked Krystyna what she had done. Krystyna told her mother what happened. The Tatar ladies gave Krystyna a tea made from pine needles and told her to soak her feet and legs in it. Soon she was feeling better.

A few weeks after the crucifix broke, as Walentyna reflected on their horrible life in Stalin's Russia, Walentyna said, "God does not want to stay here anymore."

Once again, Krystyna's mother was right.

When the weather began to warm up Krystyna decided one day to stop by the camp office. The Russian lady was sitting there doing her nails.

Krystyna was surprised to hear the lady say to her, "Sonia," (the ladies in the office always called her Sonia), "you are free to go! You can go wherever you like!"

Krystyna was dumb founded. After more than two years of hard labor, she did not know what to think.

It was now June 1942 and by this time Hitler had violated the non-aggression pact with Russia. General Sikorski convinced Stalin to let the Poles organize an army in the south of Russia to assist the Allied effort against Hitler. Father along with other still able bodied men began their journey to southern Russia on foot to join Ander's Army under the British Allied Command. All the women and children were left behind in the Urals but were allowed to find their own way back to Southern Russia. How they would get there involved much discussion, but the Polish deportees from the many camps in Russia, from Siberia to the Urals began walking, traveling in boats and in freight cars to Southern Russia some 1200 miles away. The weather would turn cold again soon so they had to act quickly before the harsh winter conditions returned.

Andrzej joined Ander's Polish Army in Exile in Southern Russia and became a cook. His unit was eventually sent to Iran. Before he left the Urals Andrzej gave Krystyna his warm coat that he always wore when he worked in the forest. He wanted to assure her they would see each other again. Walentyna, Alice, Krystyna, Teddy, Chester, and Natalie walked to the River and packed into a crowded boat filled with a huddled mass of mal-nourished fellow deportees, desperate to go home. But where was home? They could not return to the Kresy. Hitler had invaded eastern Poland and it was now the new front in the war between Hitler and Stalin, and in the conflict between the Ukrainian Nationalists and the Poles.

Conditions on the boat were terrible. As they floated down the Wolga River into the great Caspian Sea they huddled under blankets provided by the military. The children were suffering terribly from typhus and dysentery, many were dying. A Jewish man saw the blankets and asked Krystyna for one. Krystyna said she would trade a blanket for a bottle of spirituous. The man went away and came back with a bottle of alcohol, possibly vodka. He wanted to know why a girl her age needed alcohol. Krystyna told him it was none of his business and made the trade. She then began feeding the alcohol to the many sick children, one teaspoon full at a time. The alcohol helped to stop the diarrhea. The conditions on the boat were unbearable; many on the boat died. But eventually, Walentyna and her five children made it to the boat's destination, Uzbekistan, on the shores of the Caspian Sea.

When they got off the boat, there was nowhere for them to go. All around people were lying on the ground, sick from exhaustion, mal-nutrition, typhus and dysentery. Falling asleep was risky business. You would go to sleep on the ground wearing shoes, and wake up barefoot because while you were sleeping, someone stole your shoes. Soon Uzbeks started showing up offering work in the fields to some of the refugees. Walentyna and her family were offered work in a small village near Tashkent picking cotton. Food was still scarce but at least there was more to choose from than bread, water, and potato peels. Their menu expanded to include dried melon and hard cheese. The Uzbeks also made flat bread called lepioszki, in big round ovens made of clay. The Uzbeks used dried brambles for fuel. The brambles were plentiful and they would gather them frequently to keep them from choking the crops in the fields.

Walentyna shared a small yurt now with two other refugee women. Each of the two ladies had two children of their own, so now they had nine young mouths to feed plus the three women. The yurt was small, with a dirt floor. It had a large cast iron cooking pot in the center. Everyone slept on the dirt floor. The men in the village slept on quilts, but the women and children slept on the bare floor. Krystyna as always was on the lookout for opportunities to add meat to their diet. Krystyna learned how to catch and cook land turtles that were in abundant supply in the area, but she had to be careful because the Uzbeks considered the land turtles sacred and would kill you if they knew you were eating them. The eggs were big like geese eggs and they were delicious.

Krystyna's mother continued to sew and to tell fortunes, and Krystyna would steal an occasional chicken when people were not looking. Krystyna took advantage when her mother was telling a fortune to a man from the Uzbek village. She and her brothers grabbed two chickens from a shelter the man had put in the ground for the poultry. The hungry children wrung the heads off the chickens and hid them under the coat Krystyna was wearing, the coat that her father Andrzej had given to her before he left the Russian labor camp to join Ander's Army. When they got back to the yurt where Mother was telling the man's fortune, they hid the two chickens behind the huge cast iron cooking pot. One of the chickens was not completely dead and it started running all around the ground like some kind of headless demon.

Krystyna started screaming, "Devil! DEVIL!" and the man jumped up and ran away.

Mother gave the children a good whopping.

On another occasion Krystyna and Teddy managed to steal, skin and cook a lamb. They still don't know how they were able to kill, skin, and clean the animal because all they had for a knife was a piece of tin can. The land lady who owned the yurt that they were living in wanted to know who stole the lamb.

Krystyna said, "It was a Jewish man, a vagrant. He must have taken it. He is long gone by now."

At one point in Uzbekistan Teddy became terribly ill. He was so ill and frail from dysentery that they could not lift and move him

without the aid of a blanket lifted by the four corners. He was reduced to skin and bones; it is a miracle that he survived.

The Uzbeks had a large magazine storage building made out
of clay that needed repair. It was filled with oil and butter and hard
cheese for the military. Krystyna suggested that her mother should
go and help with the repairs.

Mother looked at Krystyna and said, "Why?!"

She knew Krystyna was up to something. Mother did not
know how to do that kind of work. Walentyna was a school teacher.
Mother went to the storage building anyway, to help with the work.
Krystyna went along. When the Mayor of the village came to inspect
the work being done, Walentyna was up on a ladder working on the
ceiling. One of the bricks made out of clay and straw fell on the
Mayor's head. Everyone was very serious and apologetic to the
Mayor. While this distraction was going on, Krystyna saw her opportunity. She reached into one of the big metal milk cans filled with
butter and grabbed some. She brought it back to the yurt and people
were wondering where Krystyna got that bowl of butter. Krystyna
said that she found it. All they knew was that they had butter on
their flatbread that evening.

One day the Uzbek lady in charge of the village came to
Walentyna to get her fortune told. Krystyna decided that she was
grown up enough, now that she was sixteen, and she would tell the
fortune for the lady.

The lady said, "The old witch doesn't know anything; perhaps the young witch knows more?"

Krystyna had no idea what she was doing, but she had made
her own deck of playing cards and used them to tell the lady's fortune, just saying whatever came into her head.

Krystyna looked intently at the lady.

Seeing that the lady was troubled, Krystyna said to her, "A
man who has been away for a long time will come back to the
village soon," hoping that she was saying something right.

The lady looked at Krystyna with surprise, "How do you know my son is missing? If you are right, you will have meat!"

A few days later the entire village erupted in wild celebration. The lady's son who had been missing for a long time came into the village leading a horse by the reigns. He was bedraggled and unshaved, but glad to be home. He had been arrested and put in jail for a while, but was set free and returned to his village. Suddenly everyone started grabbing quilts and blankets and placed them on the ground in front of Krystyna and placed her in the middle of them. They began bowing to her like she was a queen or something and lifted Krystyna up with the blankets and began tossing her in the air.

The lady turned to Krystyna and said, "From now on you will have meat!"

Krystyna thanked God in her heart. Now maybe Teddy would get stronger and live.

Yurts similar to the those in Uzbekistan that Krystyna's family shared with two other families.

CHAPTER 5 - Journey to Iran

Now that they had meat in their diet, it was a little easier to endure the harsh working conditions in the Uzbek village, but Walentyna was in deep thought wondering why Andrzej was not coming to rescue them. A few weeks after the Uzbek lady's son returned to the village Walentyna took a long and dangerous walk, about 50 miles, to a town to find out what was happening to all the refugees. While in the town she found out that the Russians were transporting Polish children born 1925 and after to Iran. By this time most of the deportees who had walked from the shores of the Caspian Sea to Tashkent had already found their way further south and out of Russia. Being isolated in the village Walentyna did not know that she and her children might have better options than difficult labor for little or no wages.

Andrzej and several of the Polish soldiers now in the military in the south of Russia had paid two men to go to Uzbekistan and bring their families close to where they were stationed, but these hired men took the money and disappeared instead of completing the mission.

When Walentyna returned to the village she had Krystyna, Teddy, Chester, and Natalie pack their few belongings for a journey to the orphanages that were set up in Iran by the Polish Army in Exile. Krystyna begged her mother to lie about Alice's age so Alice and her mother could go with them, but Walentyna refused to lie; she always refused to lie. So now Krystyna and her younger siblings would be separated from their mother and their oldest sister, Alice. It was bad enough seeing their father go away, now they would have to endure being ripped away from their mother, too. It was a heart wrenching decision for Walentyna. She had to get her children out of Russia before they died from dysentery, typhus or worse. Walentyna was also worried about the women they were living with in Uzbekistan. The two women were too ill to care for their children or travel; and not wanting to leave Alice alone, Walentyna decided to stay behind with Alice and to help care for the two women and their children until they were well enough to travel. Walentyna assured Krystyna that Krystyna would somehow find her father when they got to Iran, and that he would find a way to bring Walentyna and Alice to Iran, too.

Krystyna, Teddy, Chester, and Natalie were transported in lories to a port on the Caspian Sea, to a boat, a much bigger boat this time. What Walentyna did not realize is that this was the last transport for Polish orphans that Russia would allow. It was a blessing that Walentyna was able to find out about it on time for the sake of her younger children, but it sealed Walentyna and Alice's fate. They would be forced to remain in Russia. Stalin had plans for the remaining Poles still in Russia. He needed them for continued hard labor and soon closed the boarders so no more Poles could leave. The Poles left behind found themselves permanently separated from their families.

The caravan of orphans stopped at a restaurant before boarding the boat awaiting them in the port. A nice Russian lady took compassion on them and fed them all a big meal. But the children did not eat too much, afraid they might get sea sick on the next phase of their long journey. After the meal they boarded the boat that took them across the Caspian Sea to Iran. When they landed in Iran, they were transferred to another caravan of lories for a journey south to Teheran. The lories, seventeen or eighteen of them, set out for the Polish orphanage camps traveling through the seven mountains, a perilous journey on horrible narrow roads, hugging the cliffs through the ravines. The drivers drank alcohol to steady their nerves because the road was so treacherous. The lorie in front of the truck that Krystyna was in suddenly tumbled over the edge of the ravine. It broke apart in a thousand pieces and the children tumbled down the mountain side like little match sticks. Everyone in that truck perished. To this day Krystyna cannot drive a car anywhere involving mountainous terrain. The sight of the children tumbling into the ravine is burned into her memory.

In contrast to the previous two plus terrible years, Teheran was a sight to behold, exotic and beautiful, filled with wonder, elaborate gardens, mosques, sights, sounds and smells, that delighted the senses. The perpetual hunger and terror in Russia was now over, but the longing Krystyna was feeling for her parents and for Alice was soon to become her new focus.

Nobody wanted to take in the Polish refugees, not Europe, not the United States, and they could not go back to Wolyn in the Kresy because of the war. But as fate would have it, God touched the heart of the king of Iran because he had recently married a beautiful Polish woman. He took pity on the Polish deportee children. Any children born after 1925 were welcomed to his kingdom. But 1925 was the cut-off date, so while Krystyna, Teddy, Chester, and Natalie were rescued from the terrible labor conditions in Uzbekistan, Mother and Alice stayed behind.

To this day Krystyna struggles with her mother's strict penchant for honesty, often wondering, "Oh, why wouldn't Mother lie? We would still be together if she did."

When they arrived in Teheran Krystyna and her younger brothers, Teddy and Chester, and sister, Natalie, were sent to Camp Number Three. Krystyna soon became fast friends with the cooks in the Camp, the Dombrowski sisters. They were sisters to one of the two ladies Krystyna and her family shared the yurt with while in Uzbekistan. They were grateful for Walentyna's care for their missing sister and made sure that Krystyna and her brothers and baby sister Natalie always had extra to eat. The food was now better and plentiful - rice for breakfast, rice for lunch, rice for dinner, lots of other good food, too, but too much rice for Krystyna's taste. Now, seventy plus years later, Krystyna does not cook or eat rice, not even when she makes stuffed cabbage!

Conditions in Camp Number Three were rustic but comfortable. A lot of time was spent marveling at the beauty of Teheran and putting on skits and plays for anyone who would pay attention. Krystyna missed her mother and her father and Alice, but she was relieved not to have to worry about food.

One cold morning in the camp in Iran, Krystyna went to take a shower. Being young and impetuous she did not dress warm enough for the weather conditions. She was enthralled by the snow capped mountains above Teheran and in a hurry to get on with the activities planned for the day. By the time she got back to her bunk she was suffering from chills and not feeling well. The stress from the past few years on her young spirit finally took its toll and Krystyna fell terribly ill. They thought she had malaria, but she was not getting any better from the medicine. She became so ill that they sent her body to the mortuary, believing she was dead. A nurse in the morgue saw Krystyna move, signaling to the nurse that she could not breathe. The nurse realized that Krystyna did not have malaria but had pneumonia and began treating her with heated glass cups called bankies placing them on her chest to suck the poison out off her system. Krystyna recovered and was able to go back to the camp. Having narrowly escaped death, Krystyna became restless and knew she had to do something more with her life than just hang around the camp and put on shows. Krystyna was admiring the ladies in the Transportation Corps and decided she wanted to join the military. But what about Teddy, Chester and Natalie? Without Father, Mother and Alice, she was responsible for them now. At only seventeen Krystyna would have to lie about her age to join the military, but the children were too young to pull that off. As she walked along the dusty streets she thought about the situation and noticed a watch dangling in a display in one of the booths at the bizarre. She immediately purchased the watch and promised herself she would give it to her father as soon as she found him. She would have a better chance of doing that if she joined the military.

CHAPTER 6 - A Man on a Motorcycle

Teddy immediately joined the cadets; and with a little bribery, Chester joined, too. It was unusual for Chester not to want to join the cadets. Back in Orlopol Chester was full of adventure, going places everyone else was afraid to explore. Under the church there were a series of tunnels used during previous wars. The tunnels were dark and foreboding, but Chester convinced Teddy and Krystyna to come with him into the tunnels to explore. There were all kinds of relics from battle, guns, knives, and even dead men's bones. Walentyna did not approve when she found out Chester was exploring the tunnels. Krystyna offered the watch to Chester if he would join the cadets, and he reluctantly agreed.

Natalie was sent to an orphanage in Africa with many other young refugee children to keep them safe during the war. While there, little Natalie met a man, named Macheta, who was the principal of the school in Wisniowiec when they were going to school in Wolyn in the Kresy. Natalie, now eight years old, was comforted to see someone she knew from home. Africa, Australia and India opened their borders to the Polish deportees, so now the Poles were scattered far and wide across the globe because they could not go home. With Teddy, Natalie and Chester in good hands Krystyna now had a chance to join the military. Krystyna was about to turn 18, but needed to be 19 to join the Ladies' Corp, so she lied. She hoped she would be assigned to transportation so she could learn how to drive a car and be a big shot, but instead her marching orders involved nurse's aide training in Iraq. She was so disappointed, but glad to be able to be useful in the fight against Hitler and those who took away her home.

Learning from the example set by her father when they were in Orlopol, Krystyna knew that it took more than a rank or a title to be a leader. The first commander of their ladies' unit lasted only a few days. The girls in Krystyna's unit were merciless to their com-

46

manders, and did not do very well learning to march. The next commander was a soft spoken woman who did not seem to exhibit much authority either. When the girls were sitting together on a break, they were laughing at how poorly the training was going.

Just for fun Krystyna stood up and yelled, "Attention!" to demonstrate how to give an order if you want the troupes to obey.

Immediately, everyone including the commander stood up at attention, expecting to see someone with great authority pass by. To Krystyna's surprise and chagrin all eyes were on her.

The soft spoken commander walked up to Krystyna and said, "So, you think you are so smart, and know how to get these troops to listen? You teach your group how to march."

Krystyna took over the marching instruction for her group and on graduation day they competed with two other units in a marching competition. Krystyna's group won first prize. The Colonel congratulated the soft spoken commander of the girl's troupe for a job well done. The commander immediately called Krystyna up front and center, and let the Colonel know that Krystyna was responsible for the groups marching skills. The Colonel thanked Krystyna and Krystyna went back in line with the rest of the young ladies.

Around this time, July 4, 1943, the Poles in Exile heard the terrible news that General Sikorski perished in a plane crash. The Poles in Exile were devastated by this great loss. General Wladyslaw Sikorski was negotiating a deal with the Allies that would return Poland almost completely to its original borders after the War. With the death of Sikorski the Poles felt their hope of returning to their homeland quickly fade. To this day many believe that the plane crash was not an accident, but an assassination because General Sikorski would have insisted that Russia release most of Poland from its grip at the end of the war. Krystyna and five of her friends were asked to sing at Sikorski's memorial service in the camp in Iraq. Their reputation for performing was well known in the camp in

Iran and now in the military training camp in Iraq where Krystyna was stationed. One of these girls, Stefania Klimek, now lives in New Haven, Connecticut, not too far from Krystyna and they would remain fast friends for many years to come. They always loved to sing together. They would march in the back and start the singing when marching with their group in the Ladies' Corp.

One day, when leaving the hospital after a hard day's work as a nurse's aide in Iraq, Krystyna found herself being circled by an apparent crazy man on a motorcycle.

Around and around her he went, shouting, "Krystyna! Don't you know who I am? I am Walter Bura. I know where your father is. Get a pass and I will take you to your father."

Could it be? After all this time, after all they had been through, was her father nearby? Krystyna explained to her superior officer that Walter wanted to take her to her father. The officer was skeptical because so many young girls would go off to find their fathers and come back with a big belly, but Krystyna assured the officer that she knew the man from the settlement in Orlopol and he could be trusted. Sure enough, Walter brought Krystyna on his motorcycle for a reunion with her father Andrzej. Krystyna was overjoyed to see her father and leaped into his lap and would not let go.

Andrzej liked to play cards. Perhaps they made him feel closer to Walentyna when he would think about her and remember her venture into fortune telling. Usually he won when he played cards so he had plenty of money in his shirt pocket.

Krystyna eyed the bills and said to her dad, "So this is for me? Now I can buy some make-up!"

While visiting her father in Iraq Andrzej recommended that she stay the night.

Krystyna was concerned, but her father pointed to a German shepherd and said, "Don't you worry. He's gonna take care of you."

Krystyna asked her father, "What good will the dog be in this place?"

Andrzej just said, "Watch," and left the dog with Krystyna and her tent mates.

That night some soldiers crept up to the tent door to see if they could sneak into the tent and do the ladies some harm. When the men pulled back the tent flap, there was the dog sitting on guard. All he had to do was bare his teeth and growl softly. The soldiers turned around and scurried away.

As a cook in Ander's Army, Andrzej was able to put on quite a party, and from that moment on he took great care to protect Krystyna as much as he could from the boys in the military that might want to take advantage of her.

Krystyna was very pretty, and plenty of soldiers asked her for dates. She did not have the heart to refuse, so she would always say, "Yes." One week she had said, "Yes," to ten different fellas! She went to the appointed place to meet her 'dates', and soon they realized she had agreed to date all ten of them. No worries. They partied late into the night and everyone had a good time. Knowing that Andrzej was Krystyna's father kept everyone in line. Whenever soldiers came to party at the mess tent, they would all line up to kiss Krystyna's hand, and treat her very respectably. This was an old Polish custom in the Kresy. Men would show great respect to the ladies by graciously kissing their hands.

Their units traveled from Iraq to Egypt to Palestine. Krystyna felt safe knowing that she knew where her father was and could visit him on occasion.

Soon Krystyna's father received orders to go to Jerusalem. Krystyna begged her father to let her go with him, but Andrzej told her that would be impossible because the women were not allowed to travel with the men. With much cajoling Krystyna convinced her father to ask his commander if it would be ok for her to go with them to Jerusalem with a few of her friends, Stefania, Janina and

Gienia. The girls were very close and always watched out for each other. The commander agreed, so Krystyna and her mates journeyed to Jerusalem with her father's unit. Krystyna will never forget it. She had to hide under her father's coat so she would not be seen at the many check points. She even visited the Wailing Wall, one of those places where women were not allowed, and placed a prayer in a crevice between the massive stones. The Wall reminded her of the plight of her friends and neighbors in the Kresy that were long gone and nowhere to be found, especially Misha. Dear Misha, Krystyna always called her 'Stasha' which means 'bear.' They were fast friends and went to school together in Wisniowiec. Krystyna had hoped to go to the Teachers College as her mother had done, and become a teacher, but that dream was now just a memory.

When Krystyna visited the Mount of Olives with her father, for the first time in her life, she felt the spirit of prayer drop down upon her. She prayed with tremendous gratitude for having been able to see her father again, and for her mother and for Alice, wondering if she would ever see them again. The Bethlehem Grotto, the site believed by some to be the place where Jesus was born, was especially beautiful; the statues and walls were covered with gold, and glittered, bathed in the light of thousands of votive candles. Soon they would be heading to Europe determined to help the Allies drive the Nazi occupation back to hell where it came from. It was good to spend as much time with her father as she could.

Krystyna reunited with her father visits Palestine and sends a card to family and friends that are scattered across the globe in exile.

Gienia Klimik on the left, Krystyna on the right, in Palestine

Krystyna visits Jerusalem with her father's division, Krystyna top
row 5th from the left, Andrzej far right, 2nd row.

CHAPTER 7 - The Madness of War

In 1943, prior to D-Day, the Allies decided to drive the Nazis out of Rome. To do that they had to first dislodge the Nazi's from southern Italy and then from the monastery at Monte Cassino high atop steep cliffs. It was an impregnable fortress. The military campaign was ill-conceived, and more costly than any other action in the European theater of war, but the Allies had to do something to keep Hitler busy while Eisenhower organized the D-Day assault on the Nazis in France.

Krystyna's unit was transferred to Italy as was Andrzej and his division. They travelled by ship across the Mediterranean Sea from Egypt to Italy. The weather deteriorated, and the ship began to toss and turn on the restless waves. Krystyna went up on deck to see what was going on. The rain poured down, the wind blew, and the ship bounced wildly up and down in the water. As she struggled to keep her balance on deck Krystyna stumbled on a couple sitting together amidst the rigging, hugging and kissing like there was no tomorrow. For all they knew this might be their last chance to be together.

One day Krystyna was walking the deck of the ship with a navy officer. He was showing her the ship. She noticed a beautiful mosaic of an eagle, the symbol of Poland, on the wall of an office belonging to one of the commanders. When she looked closer she realized the eagle was made of red, white and silver cigarette wrappers. The navy officer stood behind Krystyna as she admired the intricacy of the artwork. He locked the door behind them with intentions of taking advantage of her. Krystyna spun around as the officer grabbed her. She struggled with him and when he would not release her, Krystyna bit his nose hard, almost taking his nose off of his face. In the middle of the struggle the officer was paged to go to the Captain's office. Wiping the blood off his face with a handkerchief, he opened a can of pineapple and told Krystyna to eat some thinking she would wait for him to return. Krystyna fled the office, and the officer never touched her again. He had a real problem explaining why his nose was in such terrible shape. Little by little Krystyna's frustration with male arrogance took deep root in her heart. Why do the men always get the credit? Why do they think they can do whatever they want with a woman? Andrzej and Walentyna raised her to be a decent respectful person. Why are so many people so terrible to each other? Krystyna still wrestles with these questions and is an advocate for women everywhere. She believes strongly that women deserve to be recognized for their contributions to the war effort, and they deserve respect for all they do to raise children and support family and create community.

On the journey across the Mediterranean Sea to Italy, they were under constant threat from Nazi bombers. The Allies made good use of metal coated balloons to confuse the German radar equipment. All of the balloons were broken by the Nazi bombers by the time the ship reached the Italian coast.

General Andre's Army was brought in to assist at the Battle of Monte Cassino, Italy, the bloodiest, most impossible battle of the European war. Andrzej was a cook in the Buffalo (Zubry) division. Krystyna continued her work as a nurse's aide in the Number 3 hospital group. As nurses and nurse's aides they received and tended the thousands of wounded and mutilated soldiers coming off the mountain in the many futile attempts to dislodge the Germans from the hilltop monastery of Monte Cassino. The Allies decided they needed to do something in response to Hitler's takeover of Europe. Most strategists know you don't dislodge an army from Italy by attacking from the toe of the boot – but that did not stop Churchill and Roosevelt from trying. In 1943 several Allied troupes from forty different countries including the US 5th Army under the direction of Lt. General Mark Clark began the landings in Italy, and in January of 1944 the assault on Monte Casino commenced.

At the tender age of eighteen Krystyna was at a loss on how to manage the men in the hospital tents. She worked with Hospital Number 3 group at Taranto, in Bari, and then in the hospital tents at Porto San Giorgio, Italy, when the Allies finally entered Rome successfully. The men were understandably unruly and difficult to manage bringing Krystyna to tears. But with some encouragement from her supervisor, Krystyna learned how to take charge and run an orderly hospital ward. She learned not to smile until the men in the tent were pulling their own weight to the degree that they could.

After a particularly difficult day, and a pep talk from her supervisor Krystyna entered the tent without a word and went about her tasks. The men started commenting on her silence. She made it very clear that she had nothing to say to them until they started doing for themselves whatever they could. When she returned to the tent she found the tent in tip top shape, with beds made and personal items put away. Krystyna earned their respect and no more did they behave in an unruly manner with her.

Some of the men were terribly wounded. The steep cliffs surrounding Monte Casino were impregnable and became a terrible killing ground as the Nazi's defended their positions from above. There was a deep crevice just below the monastery and the Nazis did everything possible to make it impossible to traverse preventing the Allies from scaling the cliff to the ancient fortress. Using mines, barbed wire, and merciless shelling and sniper fire from above the crevice the Nazis picked off the Allies by the thousands and many lost limbs and were blown apart by the mines and by the shelling from above.

Krystyna remembers one poor fellow who lost all of his limbs and was burned over most of his body. All they could do was attempt to keep him comfortable in a hammock, but nothing helped. He screamed and groaned in pain for a long time before he finally succumbed to his injuries; not even the morphine helped.

From January of 1944 until May of that year, wave after wave of Allied soldiers attempted to conquer the unforgiving cliffs. It was not until the Polish Army in Exile was sent in during March and April of 1944 that the Allies began to gain ground. Over 350,000 soldiers and civilians lost their lives in that terrible campaign. By the time the Poles scaled the final cliff in May and stormed the fortress of Monte Cassino only 300 Nazi soldiers remained, most of them so terribly wounded that they had no strength left to resist the onslaught. In response to the Nazi entrenchment the monastery was heavily bombed and reduced to rubble. The exhausted Poles scaled the final cliff and planted a quickly stitched together, makeshift white and red Polish flag, proud to have been the first of the Allied forces to enter the fortress and claim it for the West. As much as the Poles hated what the Nazis did to their beloved homeland, the Poles did not retaliate against the beleaguered Nazi soldiers left behind in the monastery. They bandaged their wounds and took them captive, and secured the area for the Allies in preparation for the march to Rome.

Krystyna's dad was a cook for the troops staging at the base of the cliffs for the assent to the front line. The only way to get supplies up to the troupes in the midst of that terrible meat grinder was by pack mule. Many a mule driver and his animal were killed in the process. When opportunity presented itself, the soldiers would party hard when they could. Andrzej was good at making sure the soldiers had that opportunity. Krystyna would visit when she could, and Andrzej expected the partying soldiers to be on their best behavior with Krystyna and her friends. General Andre's group had a mascot, a Russian bear, named Wojtek. This bear was frequently saddled up with ammunition for the climb up the cliffs. Wojtek was fortunate enough to return to base camp on many occasions for his evening night-cap, good home-brewed beer. Andrzej was resourceful and knew how to brew good beer, and he mixed a great Black Russian. The Allies did not know what to make of this strange army of Poles in Exile. They were so dapper and sophisticated and well groomed, smelling of cologne and charming with the ladies when on leave; yet they were focused, determined, and fierce on the battle field.

While tending the soldiers on her ward, Krystyna met a young man, Stanley Slowikowski, sent to the ward with a leg injury. When Krystyna brought him a plate of food he used the plate for an ashtray and extinguished his cigarette on it. Krystyna did not think much of that habit and let him know that was not an acceptable way to behave with the food she worked so hard to prepare for him. Stanley was impressed with her take charge attitude and soon they were dating. On June 3rd, 1945, Stanley and Krystyna married. They were often required to serve in different theaters of war and did not see each other that often, only on brief leaves from duty. It was not until 1947 that Krystyna gave birth to their first child, a daughter, Alice, named for her sister who was still missing somewhere in Russia with Walentyna.

Krystyna on right with Gienia in Italy, 1943

Poles raising a makeshift Polish flag on the ruins of Monte Cassino

Krystyna marries Stanley Slowikowski, June 3rd, 1945

CHAPTER 8 - Still So Far From Home

When the surviving Polish Exiles from the Kresy were released from the Russian labor camps nobody wanted them. General Sikorski's pact with Stalin that allowed the Poles to form an army under British Command was the beginning of a hope that someday, they might be able to return to their beloved homeland in Poland. Now that the war was over they could not go home to the Kresy. With Sikorski dead, Wolyn was now part of communist Russia and the Ukrainians of Wolyn did not want them to come back. When released from the labor camps in Russia the men had no choice but to join the Polish Army in Exile, and most of the remaining woman and children had to fend for themselves. Besides the camps in Teheran for the orphans, Africa, Australia, and India also became places of refuge for the displaced Poles. The Polish Army in Exile was not allowed to march in the victory parades in England at the end of World War II. The Allies found it politically inconvenient to acknowledge their bravery and sacrifice for fear of angering the Soviets. As the Cold War took shape, England allowed some of the Polish military refugees to come to England to live, and that is where Andrzej, Krystyna, Teddy, and Chester were finally re-united as a family again along with Krystyna's husband Stanley.

Natalie had amazing adventures of her own. She remembers that as a five year old she was left to fend for herself on many occasions in Russia. She remembers being terribly hungry and wandering the forest alone in search of mushrooms. When sent to the orphanage in Africa, she met a Priest named Krolikowski. At one point the Russians wanted the Priest and 150 of the orphans all returned to Poland under the communists, but the Priest smuggled all the children in his care to Canada before the Russians could take them. The Soviet persecution of the Poles never stopped and continues to this day. The teacher in Africa wanted Natalie to stay in

Africa because she was the teacher's right hand assistant, producing shows and helping with the many deported children that were not able to find their loved-ones. Andrzej and Krystyna insisted that Natalie be allowed to join them in England.

Krystyna wrote to Natalie's teacher in Africa, "Natalie may be your right-hand assistant, but she is my sister and belongs with us." So Natalie was reunited with her family in England.

Natalie later wrote a play called 'No-No Land.' It is about a witch that made a decree banning all singing, all playing, all dancing; and tells the story of how the people overcame the witch and restored joy to the land, a good metaphor for all she and the Polish people have had to endure. Natalie is an accomplished artist with a family of her own. She resides in the United States.

Teddy and Chester settled down after the war in England and both found brides and married. Chester remained in England and Teddy eventually emigrated to the United States.

The Dombrowski sisters were able to confirm that Walentyna had died in Uzbekistan from malaria, but no one was able to find out what happened to Alice. There are rumors that she went to work in a convalescent home and married a Russian, but to this day, there is no word on her whereabouts. Andrzej, finally resigned himself to the fact that Walentyna was no longer alive, and would not be returning to him. He married an Italian girl named Amelia in England in 1964. They were blessed with a son and named him Frank. Frank and Krystyna remain close and touch base with each other frequently.

Stanley and Krystyna had three children together, but their relationship was difficult and stormy. The hard drinking that went on between battles would take its toll on Stanley and many of the surviving soldiers. Stanley eventually succumbed to the emotional battle scars of war in 1949 when they were in England, leaving Krystyna a young widow, on her own, with three children to feed and very few resources. Krystyna began to teach the children in her community in England about Polish culture and dance, and put on many shows and recitals. With very little money to spend on the endeavor she made great costumes for the children from crepe paper.

After Stanley's death Krystyna caught the eye of a kind young man, Karol Krol. Karol helped Krystyna with her children, and even proposed marriage. Krystyna gave birth to a daughter, Elizabeth, during this relationship, but was not yet ready to marry again.

Krystyna has done her best to teach her children about Poland and Polish culture, teaching them about the dances she learned in the Kresy including the beloved mountain dance. Don't ever try and tell Krystyna that the Polka is a Polish national dance. It is Czechoslovakian. There are five Polish national dances: Polonez, Mazur, Kujawiak, Krakowiak, and Oberek; not one of these dances is a polka.

In 1952 Krystyna and a troupe of dancers that she organized were invited to perform at the coronation of Queen Elizabeth II. She helped to design and sew the costumes. It was an important moment of healing for her and the many Poles who struggled with the Allies to defeat Hitler, but were not allowed to participate in the victory celebrations. Even if the world does not know the truth, her children will know the contributions of the Polish people to the defeat of fascism and communism.

In 1955 Krystyna saw an opportunity to go to America with her four young children, Alice, little Krystyna, George, and Elizabeth. A gentleman that she met named Zacharjasiewicz, from the Catholic Relief Services, sponsored her so she and her children could come to the United States. They flew into New York and when they arrived all Krystyna had was the fur coat on her back, two hundred dollars in her pocket, four small children, and her sharp wit. By this time Krystyna was multi-lingual, speaking fluent Polish, Russian, Ukrainian, Italian and English with that colorful Polish accent. When they arrived in New York and went through customs,

Krystyna overheard a Russian woman having difficulty with the customs official and started translating so the Russian women would be understood. The customs official thought the Russian woman might be a spy, but soon let her through so she could start her new life.

Krystyna's sponsor had arranged for Krystyna to go to a farm in the mid-west, but he took one look at her and said, "You cannot go to the farm, you are not a farmer. Who do you know that is already here?"

Krystyna said, "My brother Teddy is in New Britain, Connecticut.

So Teddy, also new to America, somewhat reluctantly, came to New York and brought Krystyna and her children to New Britain. Teddy still suffers the scars of war. He remains in New Britain but finds it difficult to cope with what he has endured and does not like to talk about it.

Krystyna took a room in New Britain with her four children and went to work. She worked in manufacturing, studied and became a dental hygienist, and supported her family well on her own when she needed to. She continues to be active in the Polish community in an effort to preserve Polish culture and to preserve the truth about Poland's contributions during the war. She remarried in July of 1956 to a Mr. Zukian, and they had a daughter together, Eva. That relationship did not work well and after 17 years they separated and divorced.

In 1978, Krystyna met the love of her life, Ed Farley, of New Britain, Connecticut, 'a good Irish boy'. She first saw Ed at work, and with his blond hair and elfin blue eyes, Krystyna thought he was Polish. They became good friends and Ed started traveling with Krystyna and the dance troupe. They were married July 21, 1979, and have been together ever since. Through it all Krystyna has continued her advocacy for the Polish people still scattered around the globe, helping to found the Polish Cultural Club of Greater

Hartford and traveling the world with her dance troupes. Eventually, Krystyna was able to visit western Poland in 1980 a few years before the Iron Curtain began to crumble. Her Polish dance troupe participated in a huge cultural dance competition held in Rzeszow, Poland that year. One thousand nine hundred dancers came from fourteen countries to showcase their heritage.

Krystyna remembers at that time the communist regime was still robbing the fruits of the Polish people's labors to supply the Russian military toward the end of the Cold War. One night when they were performing in Poland, they walked past some freight cars filled with coal. They dug down into the coal and discovered all kinds of meats, canned hams and other food beneath the coal being smuggled to Russia. The Poles, in retribution for the theft of food and supplies that they worked to produce and needed to feed their own people, welded the wheels of the freight cars to the tracks so the train could not move. In the years that followed the Berlin Wall came down and Poland won its freedom from communist Russia as the USSR fell apart. Finally western Poland is relatively free from Russia's grip. The Kresy is still in the hands of the communists as are the Ukrainian people, so Krystyna knows she still cannot go home.

Krystyna also became involved with the Ms. Senior Connecticut Pageant, was 1st Runner up in 2001, and continues to help the Pageant efforts with organization, costumes, recruiting, and MC duties during competitions. In 2001 Krystyna's husband Ed Farley became an honorary Pole for his contributions to the Polish community.

During Krystyna's visit to western Poland in 1980, for the first time in forty years she caught a glimpse of the storks in the countryside, and for a brief moment she felt that sense of finally coming home. She will always remember that feeling in her heart, and her love for her homeland and her family. It is hard to be on the frontlines of the struggle between freedom and tyranny, but the experience has truly made Krystyna stronger. She has faced a life of struggle with determination and grace that she proudly shares and passes on to her five children, her many grandchildren and great grandchildren. Poland has much to be proud of and Krystyna's descendants will always know it because of her efforts to restore and preserve the truth about her people and her homeland. She believes in the American ideal that people can and should live together in peace, respecting one another, and helping each other. She knows firsthand that neither communism, nor fascism works, and that the grand experiment of democracy and multi-cultural freedom can work if we help and encourage one another with mutual respect, and diligently protect each other's gift of freedom. Western Poland is now relatively free from communism's grip, but the people of Poland must be especially vigilant about their long awaited freedom because of the continued instability in the region.

The Polish Embassies through Eastern Europe and now in Russia are working tirelessly to reunite Polish families ripped apart by World War II. They are hopeful that they will be able to find out what happened to Krystyna's sister Alice and many others like her that were forced to remain in Russia as the War came to a close.

I met Krystyna while working as an election official in New Britain, CT. I knew the moment that I met her that she had a story to tell. It is her fervent prayer that America wake up and take good care of democracy and freedom. She believes that the greatest threat to our freedom is apathy. It disturbs her to no end that so few people even care enough to vote, let alone vote with a good understanding of who they are voting for and what is at stake. I hope Krystyna's story has inspired you as it has inspired me to remember that freedom is not free. It requires us to be vigilant and to participate fully in this great experiment of self-governance. To preserve freedom and self-governance we must be moral, internally principled, well informed, and responsible. Government is no substitute for strong loving families.   Thank you, Krystyna, for sharing your story with us.

Krystyna is an international treasure. She is one of a few remaining survivors of WWII, a living witness to the dangers of tyranny, willing to share with us this amazing part of history. Don't ask her how old she is. She will tell you in that deep Polish-American dialect that she is thirty-eight. If you ever have a chance to meet her, be sure to let her tell you her story. You will never forget it.

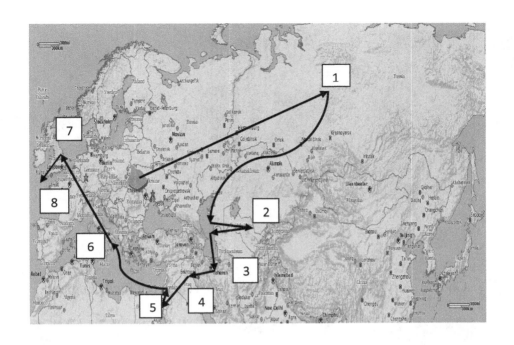

Krystyna's Journey from Orlopol, Poland, in Wolyn

1. The Urals - 1940

2. Tashkent via the Caspian Sea - 1942

3. Teheran via the Caspian Sea - 1942

4. Iraq - 1943

5. Egypt and Jerusalem - 1943

6. Italy - 1943

7. England - 1947

8. Airplane to USA - 1955

Chester, Krystyna, Andrzej, Natalie, and Teddy reunited, England,
1952

Dressed to dance for the Queen's Coronation in 1952
Left to right: Mr. Zyczynski, Helen Wasilewska, Joseph Lubecki,
Krystyna, Mr. Wasilewski, Steve Mirowski, Chris Zyczyuski,
Michael Mirowski, Natalie Rak

Dancing for the Queen 1952

Children in crepe paper costumes in England in Krystyna's Polish
Dance Class 1952

Krystyna with her children, George, Little Krystyna, Elizabeth, and
Alice, in New Britain, CT in 1955

Marriage to Witold Zukian July 14, 1956

Marriage to Ed Farley July 24, 1979

Three Kings celebration and performance at UConn Health Center
Christmas 1987, Left to Right: Dr. Jones Utuk of Nigeria, Krystyna,
Dr. I. Farrag of Egypt, Immeke Glsumbawa of Indonesia

Middletown, CT Dance Troupe, 2000
Left to Right, Back Row: Karin Gottier, Zofie Kzysz, Dona Swoltz,
Janet Jantz, Vie Bladek, Ele Nowicki, Krystyna Farley, Agnes
Destefano, Natalie Rak, Terry Dykas, Irene Kunicki. Front Row:
Bud Jantz, Nic Destefano, Ed Farley, Henry Nowicki

Dance troupe on parade

Ana Jaworski, Halina Gorecki, Clara Stawiecki, Gus Senkbeil, Jan Jaworski, Louise Stewens

Ed Farley, Honorary Pole, 2001

Krystyna glimpsed the storks in Poland on her visit in 1980 and felt truly at home for the first time since 1940.

I AM A POLE

By Krystyna Stachowicz Farley

I'm not ashamed to be a Pole
T'was thus my parents raised me
Native speech, Polish blood in my veins
An eagle forged of steel glows brightly.

As I look upon it, my thoughts rise skyward
And follow the eagle's flight
Beyond fertile fields, beyond blue waters
Along a fence where a sunflower blooms bright

Where the Wisla's deep-blue waves resound
The Polish Oberek's melody so gay
As church bells announce to the people
That the Paterka will be at midnight today

It is difficult to crush the Polish spirit
Since that's how one was raised
God, Honor, Fatherland and Love thy Neighbor
Sets ones heart ablaze.

Thus I am proud to be a Pole
I raise my flag to the skies
And thank Almighty God
That deep in my heart Poland lies.

Andrzej Stachowicz, on a visit from England to New Britain, CT
1992

Victims of the Katyn Massacre, 1940

Katyn Memorial in Bridgeport, Connecticut, with jar containing soil from the Prison Camp where Stalin executed some of the best and the brightest of Poland in March and April of 1940

Acknowledgments

Many thanks to everyone who contributed to Krystyna's memoir and helped to make it possible, first and foremost to Krystyna for sharing her story, and to dear sweet Ed Farley for sharing Krystyna, providing encouragement and space for Krystyna to take time to remember. Thank you to her five children, Alice, George, Krystyna, Elizabeth, and Eva, for encouraging Krystyna to finally get her story written in English.

Thank you to my wonderful husband, Will Knope, and to Ed Farley for helping with the taping of the interviews, and for their enthusiasm and support with this project; and thank you to Sarah (who wishes to remain anonymous) for assisting with the video edits in preparation for our Nutmeg TV production. Thank you to Nutmeg TV for making the studio and equipment available for our use, and for sharing Krystyna's story with the local TV audience.

Thank you to the incredible Jan Owens of the Millrace Book Store for providing a perfect place for the formal interview sessions.

Thank you to the Polish Cultural Club of Greater Hartford, Connecticut, for their hospitality, and to the dance troupes that Krystyna worked with over the years to showcase Polish tradition and culture, especially the following, Krystyna's dear friends from the Club, the dance troupes of Hartford, Middletown and Meriden, CT, and the Ms. Senior Connecticut group: Natalia Rak, Nelson and Krin Gottier, Ann Jaworski, Jan Jaworski, Gus Senkbeil, Louise Stewens, Helena Wapiennik, Anna Kozakiewicz, Jadzia Abramowicz, Evelyn Anderson, Carolyn Brooks, Maggie Claud, Helen Kessler, Ann Lamkins, Susan Marcotte, Grace Mills, Claire and Steve Okon, Laura Palmer, Elizabeth Perkins, Sara Pilver, Ruth Porcello, Kyle Ralston, Joyce and Gus Senkbeil, Barbara Thurz, Mary B. Turner, Vie and Chet Bladek, Nic and Agnes Destefano, Henry and Ele Nowicki, Barbara and Bill Hunt, Janet and Bud Jantz, Adel Johnson, Anna-May Maglaty, Eleonar Pozniak, Zofi and Henry

Biieniek, Jenne Janoch, Terry Dykas, George Budnik, Toni Strycharz, Olga Gorey of the Gwiazda Dance Group, Betty Fellegy, Wanda Bobinski, Betty Wiernasz, Irene Kunicki, Ruth Erlick and Eva, Claire Stawiecki, Pauline Bladek, Jolanta Marczak-Koza, Halina Gorecka, Teresa Pigula, Alicia Bartnicki, Paulina Bartnicki, Klementynka Sadecka, Aleksandra Kowalska, Michelle Koza, Magda Pigula, Elizabeth Negri, Eva Davis, Isabella Zujko, Renata Stachowicz, Andzej and Elizabeth Budnik, Regina Rudewicz, Isabelle Zujko, and Anna and Carol Oleasz.

These lovely people, and many more, all helped tremendously with the Greater Hartford Cultural Club, the dance troupe presentations, the many shows over the years, and the numerous pageants. The 1980 Polish Festival in Rzeszow, the 2001 play titled Wyrodna Corka (The Wayward Daughter), the Polish Costume Fashion Show for WGBY in Springfield, MA, and the Ms. Senior Connecticut Pageants are the direct result of these many beautiful people in Krystyna's life.

A special thank you to Krystyna's dear sister Natalie Rak for creating the beautiful story and play, NO-NO Land, and for the illustration of their home in Orolopol.

Thank you to the dance students of St. Theresa's Society in Meriden, CT, that Krystyna taught for nine years.

Thank you to Central Connecticut State University for access to their wonderful library and extensive Polish collection. And to all those deportees who have recorded and shared their experiences with the world, thank you.

Thank you to Poitr Chrzanowski and to the good people at the Polish Embassy in New York for their interest in Krystyna's story and for their efforts to reunite Polish families that are still, to this day, scattered across the globe.

Thank you to Uniel Critchley for her encouragement and editing ideas.

Thank you to iUniverse for providing a way to publish Krystyna's story.

Thank you especially to the Good Lord for bringing Krystyna into my life and inspiring the recording of her experiences that they can be preserved and shared with this and future generations for their consideration. May we all better understand and appreciate the importance of family and the gift of freedom and the need to participate fully and responsibly with love in this great and fragile experiment of freedom, democracy and self-governance.

As Krystyna often says, "There is good and bad in all of us. Choose the good."

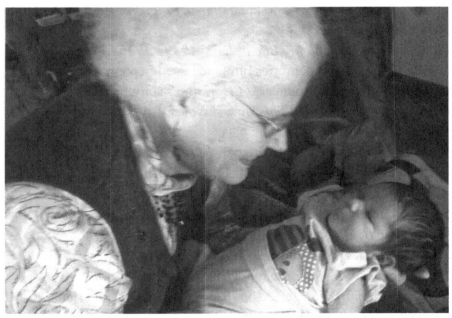

Krystyna with great granddaughter Meredith Winter
2013

Resources

Antolak, Ryszard, *Iran and the Polish Exodus from Russia 1942*, 2006

Abel, Jennifer, *An Unsung Soldier*, New Britain, CT: The Sunday Herald, May 17, 2009

DeFilippi, James, *The Mules of Monte Cassino*, A Brown Fedora Book, 2010

DeWeese, Eva, *Older Voices, an Essay about My Mother,* 1976

DeWeese, Ryan, *My Grandmother Krystyna Stachowicz Slowikowska Farley*, New Britain, CT, 2006

Farley, Krystyna Slowikowska, *I am a Pole*, Personal Collection, New Britain, CT, 2000

Gradosielska, Danuta, *My Life in Exile 1939 - 1946*, WWW.Kresy.co.uk/memories.html, accessed September 8, 2011

Holland, Angnieska Producer, *In Darkness*, Sony Pictures, 2011

Jopek, Krysia, *Maps and Shadows, A Novel,* LA,CA: Aquila Polonica, 2010

Knope, Ann, Producer and Director, *Interviews with Krystyna Slowikowska Farley*, Private Collection, 2011 through 2013

Mickiewicz, Adam, Powrot Taty (The Return of the Father), 1859

Parke, Matthew, *Monte Cassino: The Hardest-Fought Battle of World War II*, NY, NY: Doubleday, 2005

Piotrowski, Tadeusz Editor, *The Polish Deportees of World War II: Recollections of Removal to the Soviet Union and Dispersal Throughout the World*, Jefferson, NC and London: McFarland & Company, Inc., Publishers, 2008

The Hartford Courant, *A Family Tradition - Watching for the First Star in the Sky*, Hartford, CT, Sunday, November 13, 1988

Uzarowicz, Poitr, Producer and Director, *The Officer's Wife, a Documentary*, Goats Hill, 2010

Wikipedia, *Anders Army*, wikipedia.org/wiki/Anders_Army, accessed August 11, 2010

Wikipedia, *Katyn Massacre*, wikipedia.org/wiki/Katyn_massacre, accessed August 11, 2010

Wikipedia, *Wladyslaw Sikorski*, wikipedia.org/wiki/W%C5%82adys%C5%82aw_Sikorski, accessed September 4, 2013

Wolyn.ovh.org, *Orlopol, Wolyn,* http://wolyn.ovh.org/opisy/orlopol-05.html, accessed 10/19/2011

Photographs and Illustrations

Cover photograph: *Krystyna Stachowicz in 1938 with her cousin, Zbigniew Poznachowski,* Krystyna Farley's personal collection

Back Cover: *Illustration of the Stachowicz home in Orlopol* by Natalie Rak, in 2013.

All photographs are from Krystyna Farley's personal collection except for the following:

- *Yurt in Kyrgyzstan,* by Elena Moiseeva, 123f.com, Image credit: <a href='http://www.123rf.com/photo_11169274_real-shepherd-yurt-in-kyrgyzstan-tien-shan-mountain-son-kul-lake-valley.html'>olenka / 123RF Stock Photo</a>, http://us.123f.com/400wm/400/400olenka/olenka1111/olenka111100012/11169274-realshepher-yurt-in-kyrgyzstan-tien-shan-mountain-son-kul-lake-valley.jpg, accessed September 6, 2013

- *Polish flag raised at Monte Cassino,* Wiktor Ostrowski, *Soldiers from Monte Cassino,* Gadzial Kultury Press, Rome 1945, Public Domain

- *Stork posing for a photo - Poland,* by Lukas Borzych, 123f.com, , Image credit: <a href='http://www.123rf.com/photo_3469186_ a-stork-posing-for-a-photo-poland.jpg / 123RF Stock Photo</a>, http://us.123rf.com/400wm/400/400/lukejackeroo/lukejackeroo0808/lukejackeroo080800014/3469186-a-stork-posing-for-a-photo-poland.jpg, accessed September 9, 2013

- *Victims of the Katyn Massacre,* courtesy of Wikipedia, http://upload.wikimedia.org/wikipedia/commons/3/37/Katyn_massacre_5 .jpg, public domain, Republic of Poland, accessed September, 7, 2013, Public Domain